Praise for Money Sucks!

The tag line for this terrific little book captures the essence of Gordon's message: Money Strategies for Real Life. *Personal finances can be scary – especially for young people newly (or nearly) headed out on their own, or for anyone that finds themselves "in over their heads." The logical progression and simple clarity offered in these pages calms the nerves and brings the heart back to a normal rhythm. If you're anxious about any part of personal money management, or know someone who is, hope has arrived!* **Leo Muller, Executive Director, CHOICES Education Group**

Another name for this book could be "an ounce of prevention is worth a pound of cure." The best way to avoid bankruptcy is to stay out of trouble in the first place. This book is a great starting point for doing that; follow the tips, learn to budget, pay attention to your money and avoid credit cards and payday loans!! **Ruth Nelson, Bankruptcy Attorney, Seattle, WA**

A great quick guide to managing your finances; accessible to all ages. **Karen Altus, Career Counselor, Seattle Pacific University**

Money Sucks! *(I couldn't agree more!) is a great little volume on its subject. Young people just starting out on their own will find much of value here, as will parents who want to talk to their children about their new financial responsibilities and don't know where to begin. The illustrations are priceless (excuse my pun), and make the book seem more inviting and accessible; qualities that help offset the potentially intimidating or boring subject matter. Indeed, the greatest strength of the book is the little ways it makes itself a book that can be read for pleasure and in small doses.* **Judge, Writer's Digest contest**

Reviews on **Amazon.com (5 Stars)**:

Winning, Wise, Witty

This is a fabulous read for those of us who are still bummed out by our calculators. or hate the idea of budgets in general or just need somebody like Gordon to whip us — kindly but firmly — into shape. It's painless and fun at the same time. I glumly laughed at the cartoons and truly appreciate the neat ways she works out the interest payments for us. I recommend Money Sucks! *heartily, and think it's the perfect gift for graduates, whether from high school, college, or some of the more crocked ladders of life.* **Pat Hurshell, artist, writer, poet**

What we need to know...or simply take for granted

Money Sucks! *is an approachable and informative look at the practical ins and outs of money. The author is writing to young people who are just entering the world of work, saving and spending — offering what many of us wish we'd known back then.* **E. Burke, CPA**

Seven copies for seven children!

As the mother of seven children, I am thankful for this book! It is packed with the wisdom that every parent should instill in their child for life-long success — in a convenient, fun package! Ms. Gordon's book should be a part of every high school's Economics curriculum and every family's library. **Ms. Wright, parent**

Money Sucks!

Money Strategies
for
Real Life

Miryam Gordon

Cover Art and Illustrations Kaylee McAvoy

Money Sucks!

SAN 850-556X
Green Elms Press
PO Box 15186
Seattle, WA 98115-0186

Printed in the United States of America

ISBN 10: 0-9779058-2-9
ISBN 13: 978-0-9779058-2-9
Library of Congress Control Number 2008900685

Disclaimer
This publication is sold with the understanding that the author and publisher are not engaged in rendering legal, financial or other professional advice, and they assume no legal responsibility for the completeness or accuracy of the contents of this book. Laws and practices vary from state to state and if legal or other expert assistance is required, the services of a competent professional should be sought. The author and publisher specifically disclaim any responsibility for liability, loss, or risk that is incurred as a consequence, direct or indirect, of the use and application of any of the contents of this book. The text is based on information available at the time of publication.

This book makes a great gift! Contact Green Elms Press at info@greenelmspress.com or go to www.greenelmspress.com for additional copies for those you care about, to keep them financially safer.

Acknowledgements

With heartfelt thanks, I want to acknowledge several people without whom this book would not have come to be.

My sons, Seth and Magnus, were foremost, my inspiration for creating this book and the initial trainees in good fiscal habits, whether they wanted to be or not.

My parents, Bernie and Judy, continue to support the publication of this book, with a steadfastness I appreciate so much.

Finding Kaylee McAvoy to create the cartoons before each chapter was like finding gold in a corn field. The accessibility of the book is immeasurably enhanced by her humor and artistic execution.

Thanks to T.J. and Kbear for keeping me going.

Thank you all!

Contents

12 pgs.

6 pages

4 pages

4 pages

3 pages

6 pages

3 pages

3 pages

Introduction

I know that you've been frustrated by finances, confused by credit, incensed by interest rates and maddened by money. We all have. I'm going to give you the basic tools you need to tame the twisted, confusing maze of banking rules, credit scores and budget busters into a system of economic independence. You can do it and I'm going to tell you how.

I hope this guide will be an enjoyable introduction to taming the sucky aspects of financial habits. Short chapters give you the essentials that will help you. When you read these chapters, I hope you'll feel motivated to take charge of your own financial life and even research more information than is covered in this one book.

This is a basic guide to some very important concepts that every adult needs to know in order to function successfully in our financial world. So many adults get into financial trouble quickly and then spend years trying to fix mistakes. If they had good financial information before they got into trouble, maybe they would have happier and less stressful lives. I want to help you avoid all that misery and get started in a way that is successful and wise.

You may be a young adult just starting to handle your own finances for the first time. That's why I include information about filling out employment tax forms and what to expect when you look at your paycheck stub. If this is too simple for you, feel free to pick just exactly where you need to boost your money-handling knowledge.

You may have never learned how to balance a checkbook or why your credit card interest goes up so fast. You may not need the information on starting a first job. You should feel comfortable choosing just the information you need to know.

Money Sucks!

Elementary and high schools have the general job of teaching you to be a responsible citizen, but often, regular curricula don't include everyday financial concerns. That leaves you to follow examples set by parents, friends, television commercials or to fumble around learning by making mistakes. If you're lucky to have very financially savvy parents or friends or know where to find good advice, you'll also likely handle your money very successfully. If you haven't been that lucky, this is my gift of good advice to give you strategies for saving and spending wisely.

Here is the toolbox formula:

Planning = Power = Savings = Financial Health.

NOTE: Sometimes, I will mention specific percentages or specific dollar amounts. Many of these amounts are adjusted from year to year. For instance, when I detail what the dollar limits are in a "tax bracket" for 2008, this dollar limit is adjusted every year by our federal government.

CHAPTER 1

Starting Out — Adult Responsibilities

When you move into a house or apartment for the first time, you need a few tools around, like a couple of different screwdrivers and a hammer and some nails. Well, when you begin handling money for yourself, there are some basic ideas, plans and concepts that will help keep your financial "house" in order, too.

This book is a basic guide to taking care of your everyday money activity. Anyone on his or her own needs to have these basic tools in his or her "toolbox of life." If you use these tools, you will have a greater sense of security and will be far less likely to get into financial trouble.

If you're young enough that the only money you've earned so far has been from doing work like babysitting, mowing lawns or delivering newspapers, you've been part of what's called the "underground economy." You've probably received cash for your work and it's not reported anywhere and kept track of or taxed by any government.

Bam! Now, you've turned 18 years old. At age 18, of course, every person, ready or not, is legally an adult and, as an adult, is subject to all sorts of laws and regulations that governments make regarding money and taxes. As an adult, when you get jobs in stores and companies and restaurants, you'll most likely receive paychecks and will need to carefully track how much is coming in and going out.

Make a Budget

The biggest tool in your financial toolbox is going to be your budget. This is **Planning**. Instead of letting your money slip through your fingers and disappear without a trace, this tool is the way to take control of your financial situation and make it clear and manageable by you. For instance, if you're a young adult, still living at home, but you have plans to move out on your own, making a budget will tell you how much money you will need on a monthly basis and then you can figure out if you've got enough money coming in each month to make it work.

First, list all the basics you know (or think) you'll have to pay for and how much they cost/will cost:

Rent
Food
Phone/Cell Phone
Clothing
Utilities (electricity, water, sewer, garbage)
Car Expenses (gas, regular maintenance)
Other Travel Expenses (public transportation)
Eating Out
Entertainment (movies, bowling, etc.)
Medical Insurance and Co-pays
Other Insurance (auto, renter's)
Extras (gifts for self or family, charity)
Savings (or paying off debt)

Think of all the kinds of money you spend in a month, like the gifts you buy friends, music albums, paying for someone else to attend the same event with you (dating expenses), newspapers or magazines you buy, even the latte or donut you buy every week or every day.

Looking at the categories listed, "Food" could mean just the foods you buy that are staples (milk, eggs, bread, sugar, flour), but the way I like to think about food is more realistically all the things that grocery stores carry these days, which includes batteries, hair supplies, shaving supplies, makeup or other grooming supplies for women, paper plates, tissue and toilet paper, even charcoal for an occasional barbeque. That probably means you need to rethink the "food" amount you originally thought of and bring it up to a more realistic figure. You could even look at some regular grocery receipts (from family, friends or yourself) and multiply those by 3 or 4 visits per month to get an idea.

Similarly, when you think about your car (if you have one), you would want to think about what you spend over the course of a year, including fixing the alternator or replacing a tire or two, and having a tune up, instead of just the gas for one month. Divide that whole year's amount by 12 to get a monthly budget figure.

Make sure you list auto insurance or renters' insurance in your budget. Think about things that come up each year, like your mother's birthday, where you must add in items to that month's budget (and don't forget the holiday gift giving). If you usually pay something once or twice in a year, divide that into 12 pieces so you can budget a little every month for it over the whole year.

The reason "Savings" is there is because whenever you make a budget, to be financially kind and healthy to yourself, you'll need to push yourself to find a way to save — no matter what your earnings are. I know that's not always possible. I've had many periods in my life where I could not do that and have known many people who were homeless, unemployed or otherwise desperately broke. The point is that your bad financial periods will hopefully be short, and whenever you look toward the future, try to Plan for that healthy activity of saving money.

You may already have built up some "Debt." If you owe people money, whether it's family or friends or a credit card company, before you really can save money, you'll probably have to budget money to pay off your debt, as quickly as possible. We'll cover more information about how difficult debt is to handle and get rid of later.

Once you've listed all those amounts of money, you may feel like you're already way over your head. That may be true, because right now, your financial habits may not be good ones and you'll probably need to do some uncomfortable adjusting in order to live on a realistic budget. You might figure out that you don't really have the money to buy friends those gifts, or take that many people out on dates you pay for. You might have to go to the local library to take out DVDs of movies to watch instead of going to the movie theater.

Let's break down some budget-to-actual money pictures. Let's say that your list of expenses you've just made is about $900.00 per month.

Rent	$400
Food	$125
Phone/Cell Phone	$50
Clothing	$25 ($300 per year)
Utilities	$50
Car Expenses	$0
Other Travel Expenses	$25 ($300 per year)
Eating Out	$25 ($300 per year)
Entertainment	$25 ($300 per year)
Medical Insurance	$25 ($300 per year)
Other Insurance	$75 ($900 per year)
Extras	$25
Savings	$25

How much would you have to make per hour to be able to pay for all that? Let's look at two different earning pictures: earning $8.00 per hour and working 20 hours per week and earning $8.00 per hour and working 40 hours per week.

```
  2080
 ÷ 40
    52
```

What if you were working 20 hours a week and earning $8.00 per hour? Many college students are going to school and working part time and trying to make ends meet with that money. Can you afford your $900.00 a month expenses?

```
  2080
 ÷ 2
  1040
```

To find out, we need to make a calculation of your annual "gross income." That's the total money you earn in an entire year. To make that calculation, we would use the number of "work hours" in an entire year, or 2080 hours. (2080 divided by 40 hours per week = 52 weeks a year.) If you work 20 hours per week, you would use 1040 hours (20 hours per week for a year is half of 2080) to calculate.

```
  1040
  x 8
  8320
```

```
  8320
 ÷12
   694
```

Ok, $8.00 multiplied by 1040 = $8320.00 for the year. If you divide that by 12 months, you get about $694.00. You still have to do one more thing, though, to make sure you know what your monthly income would be — **take out taxes.** $694.00 is your "gross income" figure, not your "after tax" figure. The "after tax" figure is the one you actually will live on. That figure is the real dollars you'll have left in your pocket to spend.

As the saying goes, "Nothing is certain except death and taxes."

What this boils down to is that out of every dollar you make flipping burgers, bagging groceries, answering phones or working in an office, you'll need to know that **three basic taxes** totaling either 20.65 cents (10% plus 7.65% plus 3%) or 25.65 cents (15% plus 7.65% plus 3%) of every dollar will be taken out of your pay **before** your paycheck is issued to you. The next section, "Pay Taxes," tells what these percentages are and why they will apply to your earnings.

694.00
x 20.65
143.31

So, you must multiply $694.00 by 20.65%. That equals $143.31 and you have to SUBTRACT that from $694.00 to get your after-tax income. That brings it down to approximately $550.50.

694.00
- 143.31
551.69

It doesn't sound like you can afford $900.00 in expenses if you make $550.50 a month. But now you can Plan.

You could think about increasing your working hours. You could adjust your food buying and keep better track of what

2080
x 8.00
16640.00

16640
÷ 12
1386.67

1386.67
x 20.65
286.35

1386.67
- 286.34
1100.33

you eat. You could make lunches for yourself instead of buying them. You could choose to take public transportation instead of driving a car and paying car insurance. At this point, you would probably not be in a position to "save" anything, but if you're careful, you might not have to go into debt. That still means you'd be financially healthier and better off, since you now know what you need to spend to live, what you need to earn and how you might stay within your means, instead of closing your eyes and recklessly spending without paying attention. Can you make your $900.00 expense budget per month if you work 40 hours per week and earn $8.00 per hour?

2080 x $8.00 = $16640.00 divided by 12 = $1387.00 x 20.65% = $286.00. $1387.00 - $286.00 = $1100.00 in "after tax income"

So, if you have a $900.00 a month budget, and you have a job paying $8.00 per hour for the whole year, it looks like you could make your monthly budget **plus** have another $200.00 per month to work with.

Being able to list your expenses and determine how much money you need to live on is **Power**. It might not seem like a lot of power at the moment, but over your lifetime, it's the power to make choices about your financial health.

Pay Taxes

In case you missed your Boston Tea Party history lesson, here's a short explanation of why we all need to pay taxes. Governments and rulers don't "make" money, the way a baker makes money from selling bread or a tailor makes money from manufacturing clothes. Rulers have always gotten money for their activities by taking a portion of money from the tailors and bakers to pay for what rulers need to pay for. Usually, that includes services such as armies, road builders, building builders, police, firefighters, teachers and other kinds of services.

Back in the olden days of kings and queens, the rulers sent out tax collectors who could collect taxes any way they needed to, including violence and stealing. In our representative form of government, we are required to put specific amounts of the money we earn toward taxes, and then we have opportunities to vote (or represent ourselves) on whether a tax makes sense, like to raise teacher salaries, build libraries, or fix roads.

It's very true that we have many layers of different taxes. When we shop or buy food from restaurants or take taxis or sleep in hotels or rent cars, we pay lots of different kinds of taxes. Local taxes are charged to us to pay for services provided by our cities and towns. States mostly raise money for schools and courts by taxing our earnings and taxing the value of homes and businesses. Our federal government takes two basic kinds of taxes from us: an income tax and a payroll tax. The income tax is collected by the Internal Revenue Service. The payroll tax is submitted by employers to the Social Security Administration.

Income tax, the tax on earnings, is "levied" (placed on) earnings from $0 dollars to any amount of dollars you earn, even if it's billions of dollars. The percentage of tax on each dollar goes up as we earn larger amounts. This percentage is referred to as a "tax bracket."

Most of us will not get to a point where our finances are terribly complicated. Younger earners will likely earn within one of two current tax brackets: the 10% bracket or 15% bracket. That would mean that 10% of each dollar (or 10 cents) is owed to the government out of our "gross income."

IRS Publication 15 (Circular E) has a chart that shows in 2008, annual income from $2,650 up to $10,300 for a single person is taxed at 10%. Income from $10,300 to $33,960 is taxed at 15%. Income from $33,960 to $79,725 is taxed at 25%. You can see this chart if you go to www.irs.gov/individuals/index.html and in the "Search" box for forms and publications, you can type in "15." Of course, it's ultimately more complicated than that, but this will give you something to calculate with.

Those dollar limits are adjusted each year. If you know about how much money you will make in one year (from January to December), you will be able to know how much in income tax you will probably have to pay that year.

The other federal tax is the payroll tax, sometimes known as the "Social Security tax" of 7.65%. This is actually two taxes in one, part (6.2%) going to Social Security and part (1.45%) going to Medicare. These government programs help pay for older people who are too old to work and for some basic healthcare services for those same people.

The idea of this "security" system was to provide a safety net for poorer people who had not been able to save up for retirement. So, the tax is phased out as your income climbs. The Social Security portion is taxed up to a certain amount of annual income ($102,000 in 2008, adjusted every year like the tax bracket dollar limits) and then it stops. If someone makes more than that, the rest of that money does not get taxed for Social Security. When the government started Social Security, they presumed that if you were making more money, you wouldn't need to collect the Social Security money when you retire because you'd have more money in the bank (or somewhere) to live off of and take care of yourself. The Medicare portion is taxed on all income and doesn't have a limit.

The third tax, the 3% in the calculations for the previous section, is a "state income tax." Almost every state in our United States taxes your earnings. Each state fixes that amount at a different rate. For the budgeting calculations, 3% or 3 cents per dollar is an estimated amount of general state income tax. Check on your state's income tax rate to make sure your budgeting will calculate the right amount for your own paycheck. States set tax brackets at anywhere from 2% up to 6% or more of earned income.

Save: Short Term, Long Term & Retirement

We all have dreams about our futures, probably filled with things we can own or trips we can take and virtually all our dreams will cost money. If you have some extra money after paying for all your regular expenses, carefully Planning what to do with it will help you attain your dreams. Maybe not right this second, but if you can set goals for yourself, you can attain them one by one.

The most important money you need to save, **right away**, is **emergency money**. You need to have some money, somewhere, at all times, in case your car breaks down, you lose your phone, you break something, an infinite variety of things that can happen. Advisors say to keep three months of budget expenses handy for emergencies. Before you buy more things, or even pay down debt, give yourself some cushion for emergencies.

One of the **worst** choices you can make if you do not have emergency money is to take out a Pay Day loan. **DO NOT TAKE OUT PAY DAY LOANS!!!** If you don't have money this week, what makes you think you'll have more next week? You can trap yourself into thinking that this short term loan is easy money. Try everything else you can think of, instead. If you save for emergencies, you will be able to borrow from **yourself**.

So, you've saved for emergencies and now you can save for happier reasons:

- Make yourself lists of short term goals like buying a new TV or DVD player, a new car stereo or a new rug for the floor.

- Make lists of longer term goals like buying a car, buying a house, planning for the needs of a baby.

- Try to assign budget numbers to these items, so you know how long it might take you to be able to afford them.

When you have extra money in your pocket, the best idea would be to divide that money up into three tin cans of money to use: for short term purchases, longer term ones and just that ol' "savings" pot — which might become your retirement funding in time.

Like in our budget example earlier, if you actually have $200.00 a month to use and add the $25.00 in the budget for Savings (or Paying Off Debt) line, you could divide it equally, if you like, and have about $75.00 a month to spend quickly, $75.00 to put toward that car and $75.00 to save long term or save for retirement.

If you have $75.00 a month to spend quickly and the DVD player costs $100.00, it would only take you two months to save up for it. That's not that long to wait for what you want. You could use that $75.00 to increase your coffee or movie money or buy a few extra lunches or dinners out. It's your choice. Remember that if you didn't budget and Plan, you wouldn't know that you had that extra money or if you're spending too much and might end up in debt.

$75.00 a month toward a car doesn't sound like that much, but again, it's creating a habit of **Planning** and **Saving** that will help you when you have many more dollars a month in your pocket to spend. Also, knowing that you've saved up a bunch of cash toward a large purchase rather than borrowing money from a bank can give you a wonderful feeling of accomplishment when you actually do make that purchase.

Taking a moment to talk about "retirement"... It may seem so far off to you, at this point in your life, that it's not even something you have to think about. The real story in our lifetime is that very few people end up with a comfortable retirement and the best way to keep yourself comfortable when you're old and can't work is to start saving as soon as you can. Even $10.00 or $25.00 a month, now, can make a huge difference when put into a retirement savings account over 30 or 40 years.

Some retirement advice books say that you need a million or more dollars in the bank in order to retire comfortably. That's probably an amount darn few of us will ever see in our bank accounts. This guide isn't going to give you a lot of advice about how to save for retirement. There are a lot of good books out there that can help.

But I will advocate for one retirement option in a big way: Roth IRAs. The "IRA" part stands for Individual Retirement Account, called this by our U.S. Congress, and is the kind of account you set up most likely with some sort of mutual fund provider who will invest your money for you. The "Roth" part came from a U.S. Senator who helped come up with new special rules to encourage retirement savings and help people avoid having the government tax the money as it grows.

The only money you can put into any kind of IRA is **earned income**. You have to have a job, earn money and then put it away for retirement. So, if you have a big trust fund that earns interest and takes care of your monthly needs, that wouldn't apply to this.

The reason a Roth IRA is so great is that you put in "after tax" money, but then it grows *tax free* after that. "After tax" money is that money you have after paying the income tax and the payroll tax. When you're not making much money and are in the 10% earning bracket, even if you pay taxes on that money, now, over the long run your money can grow and grow and you won't have to pay **more** taxes on it later. "After tax," in this context, means after federal tax and I won't include states taxes in the following example.

If you had $1000.00 of after tax money to put into a Roth IRA, you would presumably pay the $100.00 in taxes you owe in the year you earn that money. (That's the amount of tax you would pay on that $1000.00 assuming a flat 10% in the tax bracket.)

Over time, admittedly a long time, that $1000.00 retirement investment can grow to $10,000.00, let's say. If you had **not** paid your taxes on it and invested it with "Before Tax" dollars, that means that you would **not** pay taxes on money you earned and invested. You could have saved $100.00 in that tax year by investing the money in a "before tax" retirement account. However, you would owe taxes **later** on that whole $10,000.00, as you withdraw it in the future. If you use the Roth IRA to invest $1000 and pay the $100 in taxes that year, you've just saved yourself taxes on $9000.00 of growth.

Later on, you might be taxed in the 15% or 25% tax bracket when you take out that $10,000.00. If you multiply $10,000 by 15%, that's $1,500.00. If you pay 25% in tax, that's $2,500.00. That's a lot of extra tax money you would have to pay, just because you wanted to save $100 those years in the past.

Take a look at setting up a Roth IRA for yourself and try to put even tiny amounts in there. You can start an account for very little money. You'll be proud of yourself later and glad you did.

When you put money in retirement, *forget* that it's there. Yes, it can technically be used for other things, but if you did take it out for a down payment on a house, for instance, it would be gone for its primary purpose, which is to take care of you when you're too old to work. I don't mean to suggest that you never check the account. Do keep watch on the account to make sure it's earning you money, and to make adjustments with the account if it is not earning money, but this account has a very long-term purpose which you should leave all the money in to accomplish.

Write It Down

It's very important to write down your budget. You will see your Plan, in black and white, and can post it where you will be reminded, often, how much you have to spend.

To gain Power over your finances, you must know where your money goes. If it disappears, and you don't know why, the first action you should take is to write down **every penny you spend,** every day, everywhere you spend it, just so you can find out what you do to disappear your money.

If you have already experienced problems with money, part of the problem may be that you haven't kept track of your spending habits. In order to get your life on track, you'll need to keep a written record. How else will you be able to tell where you're making mistakes? How will you know if you're keeping to your food budget if you don't keep track of the coffee and candy bars you might buy without thinking?

In Chapter 3, you'll learn how to balance a checking account. You'll be introduced to a check register, which is just a fancier way of writing down what you spend. If you do only **one thing differently** from reading this book, and all you do is write down where your money goes, you will not be able to fool yourself that you're good with money or that you're very cheap or that you know how to live within a budget, unless the paper proof shows you that is true.

You will not have Power over your money if you don't track it. If you track it, you will have the Power to find ways out of money problems, maybe before they get too big. You may even be able to see the problem in the near future and you will be able to Plan to do something about it. That is my goal for you.

Planning = Power = Savings = Financial Health.

CHAPTER 2

Getting a Job

This isn't a chapter on how to write your resume or have a fantastic interview. There are lots of informative books out there to help with that. This set of tools is for filling out paperwork when you start a job. Knowing what kinds of paperwork to expect to fill out is a good start.

Bring the Right Identification

There are two basic forms that any employer should give you — an I-9 form and a W-4 form. I say should because there will be a few, particularly tiny one-to-five person businesses that may not give you one of them — most of the time it's the I-9 form. Every employer should give you a W-4 form. If you don't get one, that business may not be reporting your wages properly, which could be a problem.

The I-9 form is also known as the "immigration" form. It verifies, on paper, that you have a right to work in the United States and have the right identification. There are two different sets of identification that are legal to provide. The I-9 form asks for either One ID or Two IDs.

Just One ID:

If you have a U.S. passport and can show that for identification, you don't need any other ID. If you have a green card, you will clearly have to provide that to an employer to show you're allowed to work in the United States legally.

Two IDs:

If you don't have a passport or green card, you will have to show **two** pieces of identification. Generally, one will be a driver's license or a state-issued identification card, with picture. The other can be one of a range of documents, such as a social security card or a birth certificate.

Section 2. Employer Review and Verification. To be completed and signed by employer. Examine one document from List A OR examine one document from List B and one from List C as listed on the reverse of this form and record the title, number and expiration date, if any, of the document(s)

List A	OR	List B	AND	List C

Document title:

Issuing authority:

Document #:

Expiration Date (if any): ___/___/___

Document #:

Expiration Date (if any): ___/___/___

CERTIFICATION - I attest, under penalty of perjury, that I have examined the document(s) presented by the above-named employee, that the above-listed document(s) appear to be genuine and to relate to the employee named, that the employee began employment on (month/day/year) ___/___/___ and that to the best of my knowledge the employee is eligible to work in the United States. (State employment agencies may omit the date the employee began employment).

Signature of Employer or Authorized Representative	Print Name	Title
Business or Organization Name	Address (Street Name and Number, City, State, Zip Code)	Date (month/day/year)

Most businesses really prefer a social security card. You'll have to put your social security number on the form, anyway, and businesses these days have been warned that they could be fined if they don't verify the spelling of your name on your social security card. So, knowing what you need to show your new employer allows you to plan. If you don't have a government-issued copy of your social security card, make sure you send for a duplicate as soon as possible. It's free, but it can take several weeks to get to you.

Know Your W-4

The other form you'll be given to fill out is a payroll form called a W-4. This tells the person who will create your payroll check your name, address, social security number, marital status and how many deductions you wish to "declare."

Many people get confused about what to put on this form and generally just check the "Single" or "Married" boxes and either put a 1 or 0 on the deduction line of the form (**the line numbered 5**). That's not a terrible choice, but you can definitely make more informed ones.

--------------------- Cut here and give Form W-4 to your employer. Keep the top part for your records. ---------------------

Form **W-4**	**Employee's Withholding Allowance Certificate**	OMB No. 1545-0074
Department of the Treasury Internal Revenue Service	▶ Whether you are entitled to claim a certain number of allowances or exemption from withholding is subject to review by the IRS. Your employer may be required to send a copy of this form to the IRS.	20**06**

1	Type or print your first name and middle initial.	Last name		2	Your social security number

Home address (number and street or rural route)	3 ☐ Single ☐ Married ☐ Married, but withhold at higher Single rate. Note. If married, but legally separated, or spouse is a nonresident alien, check the "Single" box.
City or town, state, and ZIP code	4 If your last name differs from that shown on your social security card, check here. You must call 1-800-772-1213 for a new card. ▶ ☐

5	Total number of allowances you are claiming (from line **H** above **or** from the applicable worksheet on page 2)	5	
6	Additional amount, if any, you want withheld from each paycheck	6	$
7	I claim exemption from withholding for 2006, and I certify that I meet **both** of the following conditions for exemption.		

● Last year I had a right to a refund of **all** federal income tax withheld because I had **no** tax liability **and**
● This year I expect a refund of **all** federal income tax withheld because I expect to have **no** tax liability.
If you meet both conditions, write "Exempt" here . . . . ▶ | 7 |

Under penalties of perjury, I declare that I have examined this certificate and to the best of my knowledge and belief, it is true, correct, and complete.
Employee's signature
(Form is not valid
unless you sign it.) ▶   **Date** ▶

8	Employer's name and address (Employer: Complete lines 8 and 10 only if sending to the IRS.)	9 Office code (optional)	10 Employer identification number (EIN)

For Privacy Act and Paperwork Reduction Act Notice, see page 2.   Cat. No. 10220Q   Form **W-4** (2006)

Personal Allowances Worksheet (Keep for your records.)

A   Enter "1" for **yourself** if no one else can claim you as a dependent . . . . **A** ____

B   Enter "1" if:
- You are single and have only one job; or
- You are married, have only one job, and your spouse does not work; or
- Your wages from a second job or your spouse's wages (or the total of both) are $1,000 or less.   **B** ____

C   Enter "1" for your **spouse.** But, you may choose to enter "-0-" if you are married and have either a working spouse or more than one job. (Entering "-0-" may help you avoid having too little tax withheld.) . . . . **C** ____

D   Enter number of **dependents** (other than your spouse or yourself) you will claim on your tax return . . . **D** ____

E   Enter "1" if you will file as **head of household** on your tax return (see conditions under **Head of household** above) . **E** ____

F   Enter "1" if you have at least $1,500 of **child or dependent care expenses** for which you plan to claim a credit . **F** ____
(**Note.** Do **not** include child support payments. See **Pub. 503**, Child and Dependent Care Expenses, for details.)

G   **Child Tax Credit** (including additional child tax credit):
- If your total income will be less than $55,000 ($82,000 if married), enter "2" for each eligible child.
- If your total income will be between $55,000 and $84,000 ($82,000 and $119,000 if married), enter "1" for each eligible child plus "1" **additional** if you have four or more eligible children.   **G** ____

H   Add lines A through G and enter total here. (**Note.** This may be different from the number of exemptions you claim on your tax return.) ▶   **H** ____

For accuracy, complete all worksheets that apply.
- If you plan to **itemize or claim adjustments to income** and want to reduce your withholding, see the **Deductions and Adjustments Worksheet** on page 2.
- If you have **more than one job** or are **married and you and your spouse both work** and the combined earnings from all jobs exceed $35,000 ($25,000 if married) see the **Two-Earner/Two-Job Worksheet** on page 2 to avoid having too little tax withheld.
- If **neither** of the above situations applies, **stop here** and enter the number from line H on line 5 of Form W-4 below.

The form has a worksheet attached to help you figure out how many deductions to put on the form. What you're figuring out is how much federal and state income tax will end up being taken out and sent to the IRS for each pay period. Over a whole year of paychecks, that little bit of tax in each paycheck should add up to your tax bracket amount (10% federal plus 3% state, or 15% federal plus 3% state of your "gross income").

The IRS gives payroll processors a table of tax deductions (Publication 15 mentioned earlier). The "Single" taxpayer gets more money taken out of each paycheck than a "Married" taxpayer.

Why? In a "married" household, there's more than one person living on that income, presumably, and therefore that household would owe less money in taxes, so the IRS doesn't take as much from that paycheck.

A "deduction" is used for the number of people who depend on your earnings for day to day living. Each deduction is a "person." The worksheet tells you that you can take one "deduction" for yourself and one **more** if you have only one job at a time for the year. So, an individual can choose to write down 0, 1 or 2 just for him or herself.

When you choose "0" deductions, the IRS takes more taxes from that paycheck than when you put "1" deduction or more. So, the more deductions you choose, the less tax you pay from that paycheck. Even if you are the only one supported by your income, you can still put more deductions on your W-4. How many depends on your individual situation. The IRS doesn't scrutinize the number of deductions from 0 to 9. You need to be **very careful** here to decide what you write down.

Think of this as a tax planning document for you. If you haven't made money during the year and you get a new job in October, for example, you might want as much money as you can have from each paycheck to make up for not having made money and you likely won't owe very much in taxes, since you are only working for 3 months of that year. You could possibly put

"9" on the form. If you only earn money during the summer months, you can possibly put a "9" on the form.

The tax schedule for the paychecks that the IRS creates is figured on a whole **year** of earnings. You can safely put a higher number of deductions on your W-4 for a short earnings year. If you took a job in October, you should remember to **change your W-4 form** for the next calendar year (**some time soon after January 1st**) if you keep that same job and think you will keep if for that whole year.

You can change your W-4 as often as you need to during the year. That is a totally legal activity for you to do. The payroll person must use the last W-4 you signed to make out your paycheck and must keep it on file.

Some people like to have the IRS take a lot of taxes out of each check. That means that after they file their taxes, they are guaranteed to get some money "back." If you are a terrible saver, that might be a good plan for you, since it's very risky to end up owing the IRS money and then not have the money to pay what you owe. The IRS has the power to collect taxes you owe forever and you can't even get out of that debt if you declare bankruptcy. It stays with you. (Bankruptcy is detailed in Chapter 6.)

But, if you're a good saver, you should know that any extra money that you let the IRS take during the course of a year is returned to you without any interest. The government getting a short-term loan from you and giving it back without having to pay you anything for using your money. If you are a good saver, you can plan to put that extra money into a savings account, instead, and know that when it's time to file your taxes, you'll have the money saved to send to the IRS already, **and** you'll have made interest on that money while it waited its turn to go.

So, if you're a bad saver, you'll want to put "Single" (even if you're married) and "0" or "1" deductions on that form, to make sure you don't owe the IRS anything when it comes time to file your taxes, and if you're a good saver, you can choose higher numbers of deductions, making sure that you also save money to pay any more taxes you might owe by the tax filing deadline.

Direct Deposit

There is another form that you might be asked to fill out, if you are employed with a larger corporation, that provides a service to you. If you give your employer a voided check (please make sure you write **V O I D** all over it), and sign permission, your payroll department can deposit your paycheck right into your bank. No waiting, no standing in lines.

This service should not cost you anything, but you do have to make a decision to allow your employer to have your personal checking account information. If you like this service, plan to bring at least one voided check to give to or make a copy for the payroll department. If you wish to protect your privacy and not give out the information, your employer should not force you to participate. However, there are some companies that **only** pay their employees this way and they may insist on it.

CHAPTER 3

Keeping Track of Your Money

Believe it or not, many people don't know how much money they have. They don't know how much cash is in their purse or wallet, they don't know how much money they have in the bank, and they don't know how much they spend on their credit cards.

Keeping track of your money is very important to your financial health and even your peace of mind. If you know how much money you have, when you want to buy something, you'll instantly know if you can afford it or not or if you have to **Plan** for it first. You won't have to worry about bouncing checks and you will know if your credit cards are properly paid and cared for.

What a Bank Does

Do you know how a bank makes money? The simplest explanation is that the bank makes money by having people save their own money at that bank and then the bank loans out the saved money to other people (for a fee) who have to pay it back and pay interest on the loan. But that's not the only way banks make money. These days, banks have many fees they collect, many of which can catch you off guard if you're not looking.

One bank can be very different from another in the kinds of fees they will charge. One bank will allow you to use their ATM (automatic teller machine) for free, if it's at a bank location, but will charge a fee if you use an ATM in a grocery store. That fee can be $1.50 or more for one transaction. Another bank will charge you for every ATM activity, each time. One bank will charge $6.95 a month for you to have a checking account there, another will give you free checking if you only write 20 checks or less a month. Many times one bank will have several different kinds of checking accounts with different services available and different fees for each. Make sure to ask about each kind, so you choose the best for you.

Another kind of fee, which gets very expensive and is a huge waste of money, is the late fee. If you have a loan and make a late payment, you might incur very large late fees; much larger than you think they should be. The banks like that late fee money. It adds up to a huge part of their income from people who don't pay on time.

Then, there are fees for "bouncing" checks. "Bouncing" a check is to write a check for money that really isn't sitting in the bank. Then the check arrives at the bank to be paid and gets "bounced" back to the person who was given that check. So, the bank charges you - even when they don't pay out any money - fees of $20.00 or even more. The person or business to whom you wrote the check might also charge you late fees or "bounced check" fees of $20.00 or more. You might not even be the one writing the check — you may deposit a friend's check and your friend's check bounces. **Even though it is not your fault, you may be charged bank fees.** You might as well throw money out a window for all the good it's doing you when paying these fees.

Depositing Checks

After opening a checking account by putting some money in the bank to write checks against, you'll be replenishing the money in the bank by depositing checks and cash. There are two key pieces of information that you need to manage your checking account money.

First is how to "endorse" a check you receive. To "endorse" it is to sign it on the back. If there is no signature on the back of a check, technically, the bank should not be able to deposit it into your account. For that reason, do **not** make a habit of endorsing a check the minute you get it. If you lose the check or it gets stolen, if it is **not** endorsed, it should technically not be able to be used by anyone else. If you do sign your name, make sure you include the account numbers, as shown below, so that someone can't put it into another account.

So, you've hung on to the check and now you're ready to endorse it and deposit it immediately into the bank or ATM machine. What do you write on the back?

You write your endorsement on the back where most checks say "Endorse Here." You have about one inch of space to write. The most protective thing to write on the back is: "For deposit only" and then your checking (or savings account) number and then sign your name. If you wish, you can reduce the "for deposit only" into "FDO." Placing your account number on the check helps insure that the money actually goes into YOUR account and not someone else's. The endorsement looks like this:

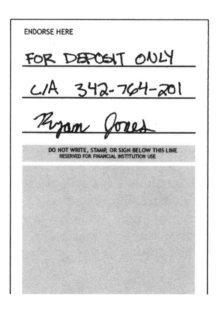

The C/A means checking account. If you put S/A, that will be for savings account deposits.

The second important piece of information you need to remember is that once you make a check deposit, that money is **not yet** all yours to spend. Many banks will impose about a two day period where they make sure that the check is cashed from the account it's written on and actually landed in your account. Many people will write checks the day they deposit money or take out cash from their account, before the check has "cleared" (meaning before the bank gets the cash).

"Clearing" the other bank the check was written from is what confirms that you've got the money. What if the check someone wrote **you** bounces? Well, your bank would be out the money you've given someone else and not yet have the money from the check you've deposited. So now, **you** will bounce a check **and** pay fees.

Using ATM machines often means the time in between a deposit and the bank allowing the money to be used is **longer** than going to a teller, by about a day. I know it seems contrary to think that using an electronic machine that can instantly tally your money transactions would take longer than standing in front of a teller, but actually, the machines are emptied and the paper checks are verified less frequently per day and so might take a day longer.

What this really means is that you're best off to **deposit** your money **earlier** and **write checks** on it **later**. Deposit money and give about **two business days at least** before you spend it. That may be a great hardship, but it will save you from any bounced check fees every time. It's worth not throwing $20.00 to $40.00 away for nothing to find ways to make sure the check you're writing doesn't get to the bank too early and bounce.

There is a way to access money faster than two business days, and that would mean going to the bank that the check was written from. If the check is written on a Bank of America account, you can go to a Bank of America location and "cash" the check. That means that you endorse the back of the check with just your name, and the bank teller can give you cash in the amount on the face. Some banks may charge a fee for this if you are not an account holder at their bank.

Balance Your Checkbook

Making sure that you don't waste your money on bounced checks leads to the mandate to keep track of the "balance" (the amount actually left) of money in your account that you have ready to spend. If you don't know what should be in your account at all times, many things can happen — most of them not good for **you** and maybe good for the bank.

Banking, even electronically, is not infallible. Machines can make mistakes, tellers can make mistakes. Mistakes can be in your favor or in the bank's favor. What if the bank charges you a fee that they shouldn't? If you never balance your account, you'll never know that you're missing money. What if the bank thinks you don't have money in your account and bounces a check you write? That's an expensive mistake, but it can be fixed. You can get your money back, if you communicate immediately with the bank and make sure you have facts to back you up.

So, how do you balance your account? To many people, this somehow gets confusing when really it's a pretty simple concept. The concept is "What does the Bank Know?" and "What Do You Know?" If you keep track of everything you do in your checking account, **you** are going to know **more** than the bank, every time. What you do, then, is determine what the bank does **not** know, to make sure you know exactly how much money you have to spend.

Here's an example:

Your checking account has $400.00 in it. You put a check in for $600.00 on March 1. On March 4, you write a rent check for $1000.00 and give it to your landlord. If you went to your bank on March 4 and checked your bank balance, it would be $1000.00. That's what the bank would say you still have in your account, because the bank **doesn't know** you already wrote a check. If you depend on **that** information and write another check for groceries for $45.00, and March 5 both of these checks try to clear your bank, then one or both of those checks will bounce and you'll owe huge fees to the bank for all that activity, because your account did not have $1045.00 in it to spend.

People who don't pay attention to their checking activity and just depend on the bank and what the bank thinks their bank balance is will likely bounce checks frequently and throw away money on bank fees. Banks give you little booklets called check registers — for free — for you to write down all the activities in the book and add and subtract every activity.

Here's a sample of an up-to-date check register:

■ AD-Automatic Deposit   ■ AP-Automatic Payment   ■ ATM-Teller Machine   ■ DC-Debit Card   ■ T-Tax Deductible   ■ TT-Telephone Transfer

NUMBER OR CODE	DATE	TRANSACTION DESCRIPTION	PAYMENT AMOUNT	✓	FEE	DEPOSIT AMOUNT	$ BALANCE
	3/1	Balance forward (from last page)	$			$	400 00
	3/1	Paycheck deposit				600 00	1000 00
1042	3/4	Mr. Smith (rent for March 2006)	1000 00				0 00
	3/4	Gift from Mom				100 00	100 00
1043	3/5	Groceries	45 00				55 00
1044	3/7	Coffee Shop	5 50				49 50

Knowing this, writing this down, you would be able to figure out that before you could write Check #1045 for $45.00 for groceries, you would have to deposit more money into the account (and maybe wait a day to use it).

Good money management takes Planning. *Planning can save you money.*

By the way, if you do have a checking account that charges a monthly fee, you should never let your account get all the way down to $0 dollars, unless you also take out that month's fee

first. The bank **will bounce** your check if they take out your bank fee of $6.95 and that leaves you with negative money in your account. If you think the bank will "see" that you don't have the fee in your account and will wait until you deposit more, you'll be very mistaken and it will cost money in fees. You're probably getting the point, by now.

Is that "balancing your account?" Not quite yet. Balancing the account means that every month, when the bank sends you a statement of the activities it "knows" about, you check the bank statement with your check register and check off what the bank "knows" about and what activities are still left for the bank to find out about.

Taking the above example, the bank statement on March 4 might look like:

United Bank

Ryan Jones
4444 Somewhere Ave.
Town, WA 12121

Bank Statement   Account Number 342-764-201

If you have any question about your statement, call us at 800-123-4567

Account Summary for March 1 through 7

Posting	Balance
February Ending Balance	400.00
March Deposits	600.00
March checks	0.00
Balance as of March 4	1000.00

The bank has an ending balance of $1000.00. You have an ending balance of $49.50. Balancing is making sure that you can make your numbers and the bank numbers the same. How do you do that?

1) Check off all the bank transactions in your check register which are the same. (See the little check mark area in the picture?)

2) Starting with YOUR ending balance ($49.50), add to that any checks you wrote after the bank statement activities, subtract from that all the deposits that you have made that the bank has not yet recorded and you have your balance.

```
    49.50
     5.50
    45.00
 + 1000.00
   1100.00

   1100.00
  - 100.00
   1000.00
```

It would look like this:
$49.50 + 5.50 + 45.00 + 1000.00 = $1100.00

$1100.00 - 100.00 = $1000.00 (bank's ending balance)

That's it. You'll match the bank! One side "balances" with the other.

What if the bank has an entry you don't, like a monthly fee you forgot? If it's something you really do owe the bank, you'll have to subtract it from your ending balance. The bank took it out and you have to take it out as well. If it's a mistake, you can immediately call the bank, have them check it out and get your money put back in. If you never balance your account, the bank will never know about the mistake — nor will you — and you'll lose money.

What about a check you wrote a month ago that the bank still doesn't know about? Can you just forget about it and spend the money? You probably already know the answer is "no."

In that example, if you wrote a $1000.00 rent check in February, but the bank statement doesn't show it getting taken out of your account ("cashing"), and you start spending that $1000.00 on other things, and your landlord puts that check in his/her bank in March along with your March rent, you will bounce checks.

Checks are presumed to be good for up to 6 months. The only way to assure yourself that a check cannot be cashed once you have given it to someone else is to a) get the physical check back and tear it up or b) to pay the bank a $20.00 (or more) fee to "Stop Check" and prevent the person from getting the face value on that check. Sometimes, banks will cash checks that are older than 6 months and even then, there isn't much you can do about it if it was not a fraudulent check. That's another really great reason to make sure you know what the bank knows and that you keep track of checks that you wrote that are floating around out there somewhere, not yet cashed.

You can even call that landlord and ask him/her to cash that check so you don't have to worry about it, anymore. Calling can sometimes allow you to find out that the check was lost in the mail or stolen or lost in someone's desk drawer. If your landlord were the one to actually lose your check, then your landlord should be the one to pay that $20.00 stop check fee so you can write another check and not have to double pay.

CAUTION: Even if you pay a stop check fee, that stoppage is still only good for 6 months. There are rare occasions where a check will get paid from your bank account after those 6 months is up, but the bank should be willing to give you your money back, if that happens, hopefully.

NOTE: Sometimes, if you keep very little money in your account and the bank takes some money out that you believe is a mistake, you will bounce checks and get charged fees. However, if the bank realizes that it's a bank mistake, a bank employee should be willing to a) take away any fees you owe and b) communicate with anyone who received that bounced check, like the grocery store and pay them back for the fees you might owe them, too. Don't forget to ask the bank to pay those store fees if the bank is at fault.

CHAPTER 4

Using Credit Cards

Credit is just another name for "loan." Every dollar that you get on credit is a dollar you have to pay back **plus** the fee for using someone else's money (that's "interest," right?). Credit card offers make credit look so easy! Just buy whatever you want and "charge" it to the card and then pay a low, low monthly minimum of $10.00 or $15.00 a month! Fabulous! What a fabulous way to **throw away** money!

How Credit Card Companies Make Money

Credit card companies are not in business to give you free money; they must make money. They do this two basic ways: they charge the store a fee for using their service, usually 2% (or more) of the entire purchase price, and then they charge you interest when you don't pay them their money back quickly. Usually a **lot** of interest — 15% to 24.99% per year interest! Or More!

So, if you buy that jersey or pair of jeans for $45.00 and put it on the credit card, the store will pay the credit card company about $1.00 to allow you to use your credit card and then you will pay the credit card company interest **if** you don't give the credit card company the whole $45.00 amount within the month.

How Credit Card Interest Works

So, you've purchased the jeans for $45.00 on sale and you got the bill from the credit card company for $45.00 and you paid them their minimum $10.00. You still owe the credit card company $35.00. This first month, they'll charge you some interest — let's say $.70.

Next month, you buy another pair of jeans, because they fit so well you need another pair and they aren't on sale, so they're $65.00.

You put that purchase on your credit card. Your credit card bill comes ($35.00 plus $.70 interest plus $65.00 = $100.70). You pay the minimum of $12.00 and owe $88.70.

The credit card company will now "compound" your interest. They won't just charge interest on the money you actually charged ($35.00 + $65.00 - $12.00 = $88.00). They will charge interest on your **past** purchases, on your **new** purchases **and on the interest you've already been charged.** They will charge interest on $100.70. That might be $1.75 in interest that month and you will owe $90.45. So now, those jeans that were $45.00 on sale actually cost $2.45 more.

Next month, you buy shoes and a jacket and charge 'em, to the tune of $220.00 and when your bill comes from the credit card company, you pay $15.00. You still haven't paid all the money you owe for that one pair of jeans and haven't paid **any** money on the next pair of jeans **or** on the shoes and jacket and you owe: $90.45 + $220.00 = $310.45. That month's interest might be $5.90 and makes your credit card bill stand at $316.35. Paying only that $15.00 minimum brings your credit card debt down to $301.35 and after 3 months, you still haven't finished paying for that first pair of jeans on sale. All of a sudden, from "$0.00" credit card debt, in three months you've racked up $301.35 you still owe and trying to pay all that in one month just doesn't fit your cash flow!

Well, that's not such a big deal, you might think.

If you were to continue to buy more month after month and only pay a **minimum** payment, you would owe the credit card company more and more and would pay higher and higher amounts of compound interest, as well. This is exactly why so many college students getting their first credit cards at age 18 and spending money on them end up owing thousands of dollars in credit card debt before they turn 19 years old. Credit card companies **love** that. They make **lots** of money.

How "No Money Down — No Payments for 12 Months" Works

A game-playing gimmick that stores use to get you to buy things is that "no money down and no payments for months" deal. Some people think that means that you can buy the item, take it home and keep the item for all those months and not even pay a penny, the whole time.

What happens when you buy something for no payments is that the store calculates each month's interest, compounds it into the next month's interest and keeps track of it, **anyway.** They just don't **tell** you that.

If you really want something on a deal like that, and when you take it home you plan to make 12 equal payments, one each month, so that it's paid off in full **before** the deadline, it **will** be free of interest. If you are even **ONE DOLLAR SHORT** of paying it off and **ONE DAY LATER** than that one year deadline, the store will charge you a **WHOLE YEAR'S** worth of interest and you will owe that too.

Example: A $500.00 couch can cost $500.00 divided by 12 = **$41.67 a month (PAID BEFORE THE 12 MONTHS ARE UP)**

OR

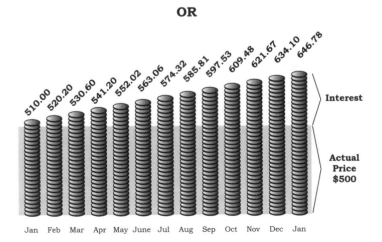

510.00 520.20 530.60 541.20 552.02 563.06 574.32 585.81 597.53 609.48 621.67 634.10 646.78

Interest

Actual Price $500

Jan Feb Mar Apr May June Jul Aug Sep Oct Nov Dec Jan

You could pay $500.00 for that couch or pay an additional $146.78 or more, even if you have paid $495.00 by the one year anniversary. Owing that last $5.00 means the store can and will add the **WHOLE** $146.78 on to your bill.

"Rent-to-Own" furniture and equipment is very similar to this gimmick. Sure you'll get nice new furniture and a new television for only $17.00 a month, but by the time you finish "renting" it, you'll have paid 3 times their worth! It would be better to go to a thrift store, buy a $12.00 chair and never have to pay any more for it. Your house won't look as great, but your bank account will love you.

The Best Way to Keep Your Credit Cards — Empty

Having and using credit cards wisely is an important way to prove to the financial community that you can borrow money and pay it back in a timely way. It's also great for you, because you can get those sale jeans before you even get your paycheck, so you don't have to wait two more weeks to have them.

If you have created a budget and know how much extra money you have saved up to buy that pair of jeans on sale and already have the $45.00 planned to pay from your next paycheck, then you can pay off the credit card to a "zero balance" by the deadline on your card statement. If you do that, you will owe **no interest**. It won't compound, it won't build up, and you will be able to say, "I bought these jeans on sale" and mean it.

Manage Your First Credit Card

You might be bombarded with credit offers with instantly usable credit cards. If you want to begin trying out a credit card, picking **one** of the offers (hopefully with no "annual fee" that the credit card company charges you just for using their card), might be the way to go.

Another way to get started with a credit card is to apply for a "secured" credit card. To "secure" your credit, the card company demands a deposit of $100 or $500 to begin using the card, and the company expects you to pay back all the charges on that card in **EACH** month. You use your own money, similar to a checking account, until you have a good track record of paying your card properly. After awhile, you can request that the credit card company increase your credit limit beyond the money you've "secured" with them. This could be a good way to get good credit habits from the very beginning.

The safest thing to do with credit cards is to use them just like your checking account. You can even take one of those free check registers from the bank and write down all your credit card purchases each month to keep yourself on track. Make sure you have the cash to pay the credit card off **each month** or keep it empty if you're not good at keeping track of deadlines.

Keep Your Receipts

The receipts you receive at the store at time of purchase are very important to match to the credit card company's statement. If you know you purchased all those items, you can be secure that a) you owe all that money and b) only you are using your card. If there are more items on that statement, maybe someone has stolen your card or your identity. I talk more about stolen identities in Chapter 7. Also, the credit card company may have placed something on your account that doesn't belong. Check the statement at least once each month.

If you play the credit card game **your** way, you'll use the credit card company's money and never even have to pay a fee for it. If you play **their** way, they win big every time.

CAUTION: Interest rates on your credit card can **instantly go up without notice** if you pay **another** credit loan late! This is called "universal default." If you miss a car payment, your ***credit card interest rate can immediately go up, even though you never paid one late payment to the card!*** Be aware!

CHAPTER 5

Knowing Your Credit Score

As you use credit cards, you start building a "score." When you pay your credit card on time, the credit card company sends a report to one, two or all three national credit reporting agencies: TransUnion, Experian and Equifax. These companies use that information to build a file on your spending habits. Using a formula developed by Fair, Isaac & Company (FICO) and used nationally, you are scored on how well you pay your credit back over time.

There are some great web sites that can give you lots of information about your credit score and you can even find out what your personal score is by going to some free sites. One of the sites I found a lot of information at is **www.howstuffworks.com**. Fair, Isaac & Company has a site at **www.fairisaac.com** and provides personal FICO information at **www.myfico.com**.

Below is a chart copied from myfico.com that shows a score range, an interest rate and a payment per month. This is one you would use if you were buying a house.

Your FICO Score	Your Interest Rate	Your Monthly
720-850	5.433%	$851
700-719	5.813%	$862
675-699	6.151%	$914
620-674	7.301%	$1,026
580-619	8.631%	$1,167
500-559	9.239%	$1,238

You can see that the higher your FICO score, the lower the interest rate could be offered to you and the smaller your monthly house payment would end up. That could save you lots of money over time.

If your habit is to pay late, the credit card company would send that information and your score would get lowered. You can see that as your score goes down to 682, you could end up paying $63.00 a month more and it gets worse as the score gets lower.

The lower score means that you might get turned down when you try to get that car loan or house loan. Once you have turned 18 years old, you are considered an adult and everything you do to your credit stays with you for an incredibly long time. If you screw up when you're 18, it could haunt you until you are in your mid-20s, even if you fix a lot of bad habits over time.

How to Have a Good Score

I know you're beginning to see a pattern, here. If you make a budget, pay your bills on time, pay off most or all of your credit card charges each month, you should build a great credit score. Those web sites and others give great advice on other ways to make your score as good as it can be.

Paying your rent on time or paying your phone bill on time does **not** help your score and that seems discriminatory. The credit reporting agencies have not developed a way to collect that information and use it to factor how good a bill payer you are. There appears to be a welcome movement to develop a national reporting service for utilities and rentals, which could help many lower income people get much better scores and better rates when they borrow.

What Makes a Bad Score

Obviously, paying your bills late or not at all is a great way to lower your score. Other ways are less obvious. You might have too many credit cards sitting around. Even if you don't use them, sometimes your score is lowered due to "too much credit." If you do get in trouble paying rent, sometimes that *is* reported to the credit agencies and that will also hurt your score. Bouncing checks is another bad way to lower your score, which is another negative activity that gets reported by banks.

There are other items people may owe that also get listed on a credit report like child support payments or federal student loans. These items can add to your score if you are on time with payments or lower your score if you are slow paying.

Again, there are more activities that tend to lower your score and much has been written about this topic and posted on the internet.

How to Fix Problems

Once you have made some bad moves and realize that you're hurting yourself pretty badly in the process, you can change your habits and work on getting your score back up to where it will help instead of hurt you.

Every year, you should make **a habit of getting your Free credit report** from **each** of the credit reporting agencies. (See the Addendum for addresses and web sites.) Make sure all the information on each report is exactly correct. Knowing what information is being passed around about your financial health is one very important piece of Planning Power.

There are "credit repair" agencies. Some of them are non-profits, some of them are not. Some of them are scams, some of them are not. These services are **not free**. Do some checking around before you use an agency to make sure the agency is a good one for you to use.

Beware, particularly, of credit repair agencies that promise **LOWER** monthly payments and quick debt retirement. There is really nothing "quick" about getting out of debt, unless you suddenly win the lottery! It took you some time to get into this debt, and it's going to take you time to work yourself out of it.

Web sites listed at the back of the book for consumer information can be ways to find people to help you or books to read. You can fix your credit all by yourself if you learn how.

One action you can and should take, immediately, is to start paying your credit card bills **on time** with **at least** the minimum payment. You don't get extra credit for paying your bills early, but it might help YOU feel more in control of the situation.

Calling places that you have paid late to is another avenue to try (**except** for credit card companies - see Page 46). Especially after you have changed your ways for five or six months, you can call that doctor's office, for instance, and see if they will report something positive to the credit reporting agencies. It won't take away the late payments, but it might be good to add to your report.

If you bought something on payments from a store, got behind but finally paid it all off, ask that store to write a positive statement to the credit reporting agencies.

You can also write things into your credit report. Sometimes credit reporting agencies get things **wrong.** Especially if your name is John Smith or something very common, you must be sure all the information belongs to **you**. They could have put information from another John Smith into **your** credit report.

When credit reporting agencies have something wrong in them, they are supposed to correct it. However, this can be a long, difficult process at times. If you want to make your own statement about a wrong item or how you corrected a bad habit or how you were unemployed for awhile, but now you have a steady job and have shown that you pay bills on time, you can send that statement in to the credit reporting agencies and they are **required** to include that so lenders will have the statement to read in your file when you apply for credit and they look at your file from the credit reporting agency.

CHAPTER 6

Paying Late —
Only When You Have To

There are probably only a handful of people who never ever get into financial trouble. We all have bad spots or times when maybe we're going to school and living on very little. Even during these tough moments, you can try to manage your financial health the best way you can. One of the best ways is actually to **communicate** with your creditors (the people you owe money).

You may have heard people say that "many people are one paycheck away from the poor house" or some similar statement. Banks, credit card companies, stores and utility companies are used to people having a hard time, once in a while.

You've probably seen at least one movie where a guy who wants a drink goes up to a familiar bartender and asks the bartender to put that drink on his "tab." The movie doesn't show a whole lot about the relationship between the drinker and the bartender, but if the bartender gives the guy a drink, you can make an assumption: The guy has probably done this before and has probably paid the bartender what he owed in the past.

Lots of smaller stores and neighborhood stores are places that may do you favors if they have gotten to know you and think they can trust you. It can be part of our "helping community" to have places that will let you have a meal or drink or bag of groceries without paying when you're having money trouble.

Tell People You Owe Money To That You Will Be Late

It may feel embarrassing or uncomfortable to let someone know that you can't pay what you owe right now. It's not a fun conversation. The surprising part is that if you do make that contact, your creditors may surprise you with tolerance. Most people who owe money don't make any call at all and they just get more and more behind.

Unfortunately, this tolerance is **not applied at credit card companies**. (This is another reason to limit any credit you carry and to manage only one credit card rather than many.) If you are late and you call a credit card company, you might trigger "Universal Default" (see Page 37) and the interest on all your credit cards and car loans might go up.

Many of your local companies and service providers will work with you if they are called early on, instead of being ignored. First of all, Plan to contact someone **before** you are late. Having a note in your record at the telephone or cell phone company, calling ahead of time, can be the difference between having your service cut off and keeping your link to the outside open. Late fees of $20.00 or more are commonly charged on top of interest, and if you call ahead of time, you may still owe interest, but maybe the representative on the phone will "waive" (not charge you) the late fee. Once you've missed a payment or two and not told the company, a service representative isn't going to feel like helping you out very much.

Next, try your hardest to send **something**. You may have a $100 bill to pay, but if you say you'll send $10.00 and that's all you have, but you'll send $10.00 more in a week, that's going to go over better than saying you can't pay anything at all. If you can't pay anything at all, try to make a Plan for when you **CAN** pay something. You may feel pressured by the service rep, but realize that trying to get you to pay is part of his/her job. The service rep doesn't really know you and why you can't pay. The service rep has probably been told lots of stories.

The point is: what you tell the service rep usually gets written in your file for the next service rep to read. The next time you call or pay, the notations will show these contacts.

Also, write down the date you called and spoke to someone, the person's name and that person's phone extension or contact number. If you make a list of dates and contacts, the next time you call and say "Debbie at Extension 336 said on March 4, 200_, I could send $10.00 last week and $10.00 this week. Do you have that in the file?" and a rep can confirm seeing that note, you'll be in much better connection with the creditor.

Keep Your Word

The next most important step is to **keep your word**. You're making a verbal contract with a person about your actions. You've already broken the original agreement (paying the whole bill), so your next set of actions and agreements must be kept in order to have the best financial health you can have.

If you made that agreement to send $10.00, do everything you can to actually take that step. Even if you have to call back the next week and say you can only send $5.00 that next week, you will show that you're trying hard to be honest and true to your word. Creditors are very impressed with that kind of forthright and take charge behavior. Of course, if you have to call back and change your last agreement, please apologize to whomever you speak with. Remember, they don't have to do you any favors and still can turn off your service or charge enormous late fees.

Know the Consequences of Bad Money Handling

You already know that missing credit card payments can get you lots of late fees, put your utilities or credit cards in danger of being turned off and lower your credit score.

Having a low score may even stop you from:

• getting a job you want

- getting an apartment you want to rent
- getting a car using credit payments
- finding financing to buy property (your potential home)
- getting charged higher premiums on all your insurance policies

You can guess that paying your rent late or not at all can get you evicted. Realize that many bad credit incidents stay listed on your credit report for a long time, even when you try to change your habits.

Some people around you may have chosen to "declare bankruptcy" and you see them relieved that they no longer owe all that money. More and more people, especially younger people who get into early credit trouble, are declaring bankruptcy. Below, I'll describe why this option should only be considered after you have worked hard to correct your spending and saving habits.

If you or some you know declares bankruptcy and doesn't change the behaviors that get you into trouble in the first place, you can find yourself even worse off than before. This information is only to help you understand how difficult it can be if you get into these kinds of heavy debt.

There are some debts that declaring bankruptcy may **not** wipe clean. Two financial debts that will probably not be wiped clean by bankruptcy are past due child support and unpaid federal student loans. These are two debts that you most likely will be required to pay until they are paid off. Being poor or unemployed or not making a lot of money will not be reasons to reduce those debts. Unpaid student loans have caused major headaches for young people who haven't paid them and want to get other kinds of loans, like car loans.

Child support levels are supposed to be adjusted due to changes in economic circumstances, but in order to change any court order, you have to go back to court. You probably need to get legal help for that, as well. This will also cost money.

Stay Away From Bankruptcy

Essentially, to be bankrupt is to owe more in value than all of what you own. You're so broke you can't catch up, even having changed your habits and "consolidated your debt" (transferred all your debt to one card for an easier monthly payment — one of the things credit counselors often help manage).

Bankruptcy declaration isn't just filling out a form and then you don't owe anyone money. It's a complex legal procedure. Judges, courts and other people get involved in your personal finances in a big way and they tell you what to do. You lose control over the proceedings. The action of filing is demonstrating that you aren't able to properly control your spending, so the government has to do it for you.

It also **costs you money to do this.** Lawyers are needed to help you file bankruptcy and those lawyers know you're broke, so you have to pay them their money up front (before they will work for you).

Our federal government has passed laws about how we legally declare we're broke. You can find those rules in the section of laws of the United States Code called "Title 11: Bankruptcy."

Under that Title, you can find different "chapters" for different ways to declare that you're broke. The two chapters that apply to most situations are called Chapter 7 and Chapter 13. These chapters are each a different kind of bankruptcy action.

Chapter 7 is called "liquidation." Everything you own that can be sold is turned into "liquid" cash to pay back your debts. You will be allowed to keep basic things like your clothes and even a house, but non-essential valuables (expensive jewelry, art, a second vehicle - like that motorcycle you dreamed of and just purchased) must be sold. After liquidation, your cash is then offered to each of your creditors to pay your debts. The offer is only a small percentage of the money you owe to "forgive" (pay off) your bill.

A Chapter 13 bankruptcy is called "an adjustment of debts of an individual with regular income." You have to already have a regular job to use Chapter 13.

Bankruptcy will affect your credit for years to come. You may not be able to buy a car or home or large appliances without a great deal of trouble after a bankruptcy. What do I mean, particularly, by "a great deal of trouble?" The biggest result is that the interest rate on *all* your purchases, **everywhere,** will go through the **roof**. You'll also pay more on premiums for insurance on cars and even your health.

Often, people get offers for more credit cards right after they file for bankruptcy! Why? Because the credit agencies know these people can't file for bankruptcy **again** and so the credit card agencies won't lose their money this time! They really don't care how much trouble you have handling money, as long as they get to keep collecting it. They are very happy to charge you **much higher interest rates** after bankruptcies to make a lot of money off you.

People with bad credit records pay a high price, literally, for these mistakes. Instead of getting a preferred low interest rate, like 15%, these people will be charged 24%, 27%, more. Let's get *more* elemental:

If you owe $100 and are charged 15% interest, you will pay $115. If you are charged 27%, you will pay $127. If you owe many hundreds or thousands of dollars, that extra $12 per $100 can result in hundreds or thousands of additional dollars it will take to pay off the debt.

Going back to the discussion in Chapter 4 about credit cards compounding their interest, you could be paying $12 dollars more per $100 on top of your $12 more interest from **last** month! You're not paying interest on an actual *product* anymore, now you're paying interest for not paying off your *interest*!

That actually happens in *any* month where you don't pay your credit cards in full each month, but the higher the interest rate, the harder it is to get rid of the debt, and the more interest you pay for not paying all your interest. People who have bad credit will continue to be made poorer by being charged more to borrow. This is part of the "cycle" of poverty and why there is a saying, "the poor keep getting poorer."

Credit reporting agencies are supposed to keep records of your credit history for the most recent 7 years. They keep bankruptcies on your report for 10 years. You might think that your bankruptcy won't show after that time. That assumption could be wrong and you may find that the credit report will still contain the bankruptcy information longer.

This is another reason to fix your credit in other ways than bankruptcy. If you finally pay off your debts, without declaring bankruptcy, you won't have a black mark on your credit record for 10 years. It will be erased after 7.

Research Your Bankruptcy Options

If you have already gotten into the situation where you feel you can't dig out by changing your habits and paying off what you owe, you may be ready to explore bankruptcy, even knowing all of the above. For some people who have gotten so deeply in debt, bankruptcy is the only option.

No matter how desperate you feel, do take some time to research your options. Many bankruptcy attorneys will extend free initial consultations. Take the time to "shop" for an attorney, just as you would for a good financial professional or a doctor or a school to enroll in. Make sure you feel that your attorney will be approachable, clear, and give you the advice you need.

Obviously, I'm hoping you'll never have to go through any kind of bankruptcy **in your lifetime!**

CHAPTER 7

Saving Through Better Shopping

Buying stuff is a lot of fun, especially when you start making your own money and choosing to how spend it. Clearly, budgets can help you figure out if you have the money for the item, but good financial habits should include learning to be a good shopper. A good shopper learns to watch for sales, cuts coupons, explores local stores to compare prices in each and keeps himself/herself from "impulse" buying and taking stuff out of a store that he/she didn't plan to buy that day.

Research When You Can

One technique that can help save money and prevent impulse buying is research. Almost anything you see in a normal department store or catalog is duplicated in many other stores. Brand name companies don't just sell to one store; they sell to multiple locations and you can buy that same exact model from multiple locations. Taking the time to research can get you the exact same item for at least a little less and sometimes **much less**.

Let's say you'd like a stereo system and have gone to a department store to look around. You've asked the salesperson a bunch of questions, like "does it matter if a stereo system is cheaper — does a higher price mean a better quality?" and "do you know if there have been a lot of returns of this model to the store?" and "is this system compatible with machines I have already?" and "do I need all the buttons on this or can I be happy with fewer options?"

Either that salesperson or another has answered your questions and you have knowledgeably chosen your preferred model or models. Remember that no salesperson can **make** you buy something because you asked a bunch of questions! Write down the brand name and model number of any items you like and want to research further. Maybe there are two or three models that look about the same to you. Then, **go home**.

With internet access, you can:

- look up the manufacturer and compare models

- do price comparisons to see what it would cost from an internet store as compared to the brick-and-mortar store you asked questions at

- go to the library to look at magazine articles about stereos in Consumer Reports Magazine, for example, to determine if your chosen model is a good buy or breaks a lot

If you're just a little patient and give some effort toward this kind of checking, you can get the best system your dollar can buy, at the best price you can find for it. Maybe that tv you thought you wanted for $420.00 isn't the best brand and you can find a really great one for $100.00 less. On your budget, look how much faster you can save to buy it!

Look at Labels

Did you think that the largest size box of something is always the cheapest? Well, of course it's not — at least not always. Grocery stores are now mandated to post the "per ounce" (oz.), "per hundred", "per pound" (lb.) or per "each" price on their items, along with the price for the whole box, bottle or jar. That little tiny printing can mean the difference between spending $1.00 more or $1.00 less. **But!** Remember that store personnel make those mathematical calculations and they may be terrible at math! Look at the "per" price and do your **own** calculation to make sure it's correct!

A great example is Cheerios. For years, there were 3 sizes of Cheerios boxes on the shelves. There was a 10 oz., 15 oz. and 20 oz. box (now they weight less). I always look at the "per oz." price, just to make sure I know what the cheapest box is **today**. It used to be — guess which? The **middle** size. These days, the middle and large sizes are about identical. But any given day, one box might be a better buy than the other. Many times, sales on smaller sizes make them better buys than larger sizes, at that moment.

You know that there are "store brands" that can often taste almost exactly, if not exactly, the same as the brand name food. How about store brand clinging plastic wrap? Charcoal? Paper plates? Bandages? Lots of "store brand" items are cheaper and so identical that it's kind of crazy not to buy them. Most of what you pay extra for in the brand names is the advertising they spend.

At least you can experiment, cheaply, and try a store brand package one time. If you don't like it, you can go back to the brand name stuff. If you like it — one more victory for your pocketbook.

If you have figured out that one local store has cereal and hotdogs at the best price and another usually has soup and bread at the best price, and you can make the time for two stops, that's another way you'll help yourself save. If you have never tried using those newspaper coupons, you'll truly be surprised at the idea that someone would give you a dollar to buy an item you were going to pay full price for anyway. This can be lots of fun. Whole books have been written by people bragging how they used coupons to do hundreds of dollars of buying at once and only paid $4.96 for all of it!

Many More Ways to Save

Another tool for saving money when you buy can be to research a purchase and then wait for the sale on it. Winter time holiday sales either before or after Christmas are great times to make purchases on electronic equipment. It's always discounted then, it seems. So, if you wanted that digital camera and figured out the best brand and model, you might save over 25% of your costs if you can get yourself to wait for the best sales.

A word about "extended warranties:"

Many electronic items are sold in stores with "extended warranties." The extension is beyond the limit of the "manufacturer's warrantee." The manufacturer will warrantee the item not to be defective or break for a set period of time, usually 90 days, 6 months or a year. Stores push their salespeople to sell extended warranties to you, so that if something breaks after 18 months, you can still return it and get a replacement without paying for a whole new item. Almost all defects show up in the manufacturer's warrantee period. The extended warranties are **rarely used** and store owners know this, so mostly they are just making extra money on your sale. Think carefully before you buy one. Consumer Reports Magazine, for one, has even done research on what kinds of extended warrantees are useful and which might not be.

Another important action:

Many people advise making a shopping list when you go to the grocery store. Stores know that attractive displays make it easy to impulsively buy things you didn't think you needed. That's one of the ways they make more money when you visit them. If you think about your shopping needs before you get to the store, you'll be less likely to look at pretty displays and buy something you really didn't think you needed.

Also, it's really **not** very effective to go to the grocery store **hungry**. Guess what? **All** the food looks so much better and you want much more of it and will impulsively fill your cart. Do yourself a fiscal favor and eat a little something before you go to the store.

One more tip has to do with food waste — buying something and not using it up and it spoils. That actually costs us (collectively) a ton of money each year. **Check the expiration dates on your food before you put it in the cart.** If you buy the newest milk and cheese and freshest fruit, it will last a day or two longer at your home.

Try buying in bulk (large quantities) and divide it up at home and freeze some for later. Larger quantities from "warehouse" stores like Costco can be a savings over time. You do have to pay a bit more for the large quantity, but often it's significantly cheaper per pound or ounce (or each) and lasts a long time.

Of course, there are other tricks and tips for saving when shopping, but I hope this gives you a good start in that direction. A few dimes and nickels later, you've actually saved a dollar and that dollar can add to others.

.

"BRANDON'S LOW-TECH SHREDDER"

CHAPTER 8

Keeping Your Personal Information Safe

You've probably heard about people having their "identities" stolen. This is a new kind of crime in the era of so much computerized information. We do a lot of business without ever meeting each other these days.

When your identity is stolen, what that really means is that someone has pieced together some vital personal numbers and used them to fraudulently make purchases, get loans, get new cell phones, and other sorts of stealing using your name. While this kind of crime is happening more and more, it is still very hard to stop and to fix.

The pieces of information people generally need in order to pretend they are you are: your social security card, your address, and your birth date. If they can find out your telephone number and credit card number and the extra three digits printed on your credit card, known as the "security code," they're doing even better.

When they charge things on credit cards with your name on them and don't pay, when they open accounts at stores and don't pay, when they obtain drivers' licenses in your name and have accidents with no insurance, the credit reporting agencies report all that on **your name**.

You become the one with the bad credit score and police often can't even identify who's the real criminal since the crime is committed electronically. Stories have been reported that it takes an average of about two whole years to finish clearing up the problems and credit reporting errors that accumulate. Most likely, one of the things you will end up having to do is to ask for a new social security card with a new number and get lots of pieces of new identity. You will be the one to have to start over. The criminal can just move on.

Even Children Have Their Identities Stolen

Identity criminals have gotten so good at finding this kind of information that even newborn babies are at risk of having their identities stolen, almost from the moment of birth. Once a newborn has a name, social security number and a birth date, credit can be established in his or her name. Children aren't supposed to be able to have credit (since the law protects them from having to pay back debt in many cases), but somehow the birth date gets altered and away the criminals go.

Then, when children get old enough to begin to establish credit in their own names, they find that someone has been there before them and it can be years before that child or young adult can function normally with their own credit. Identity theft often makes the victim feel like a criminal, since it's so hard to show that you aren't you, electronically.

Several Ways to Be Safer

Following all the steps I will outline here still cannot guarantee that you will never be the victim of identity theft, but these are all simple steps that don't take a lot of time and will help you keep your identity safe.

There is a new option the credit reporting agencies are now allowing: you may "freeze" your credit! This means no one, not even you, can get **new credit** until the freeze is taken off. So, if you freeze your credit (or your **child's** credit), if you want to buy something at a store and use a new store credit card, you'll have to unfreeze your credit, first. But that means that **no one else** can get new credit on your account, so that is the safest option. This option used to be available **only** to those whose identities were already stolen, but that was like shutting the barn door after the horses were already gone. This is a huge, and welcome, action on the part of the credit reporting agencies.

Each state has different regulations regarding freezes. The three reporting agencies have pages on their web sites about how to put on a "security freeze." In most states, you will pay a fee of $10 to **each** of the credit reporting agencies to freeze your credit. This equals $30.

To UNfreeze your credit, each time you *want* to have new credit added, will also cost $10, possibly also to **each** credit reporting agency. (This is not clear at the time this is written.) But when you think about it, you might have two credit cards and a gas card, for instance. You should not have to unfreeze your credit very often, once you have established what accounts your lifestyle calls for.

NOTE FOR PARENTS: Consider putting a freeze on each of your children's credit. For $30 ($10 to each credit reporting agency), one time, until they're old enough to have credit (perhaps age 15?), you can stop anyone from opening new credit accounts on your children's social security numbers and names. $30 is very cheap for the peace of mind you get protecting your children and knowing their credit record is safe.

More Steps:

Never let a piece of paper with your personal numbers on it, linked to your name, **ever just be left behind or thrown away** in a common garbage area. There are many pieces of paper that you **must** fill out and have to trust that the people you give those papers to will be careful with your information. You can't help that.

There are ways to minimize giving out personal information. Your birth date is not really something you should let people write down and keep, except for places like doctors' offices, and on employment forms like the I-9. The U.S. government has said that your social security card should not be considered a "national identity number," but many entities, including banks will ask for that number anyway. Since the U.S. Congress passed a newer federal law for preventing terrorism, called the "Patriot Act," the social security number is almost a "de facto" (in fact) national identity number. Try to avoid giving any numbers out unless you feel you must. It's much harder to avoid than it was a while back.

Keep all credit card receipts and take them home and shred them. Use paper for burning in the fireplace. Tear it up. Just don't take it for granted that someone won't use it.

Keep all paperwork copies from the doctor or work and do the same. If you keep paperwork for a year or two or three, like tax returns, when it's time to get rid of it, don't just throw it in the garbage or recycle! *Shred, tear, burn*.

Be careful of the information you give anyone on the phone (cell phone included). If someone calls **you** and asks for information, **don't give it**. Ask for a number to call them back at so you can verify if they are who they say they are. Many people are scammed on the telephone. Banks do **not** call you and ask you to verify your pin number on the telephone. Credit card companies do **not** call and verify your credit card number. They also don't send emails asking you to verify these numbers! This is a computer scam called "phishing."

If you have called an "800" number to buy something, be sure to ask that your name not be put on a mailing list that is sold or given away. This not only stops junk mail, but can help keep your identity safer. Using the internet to purchase items can be very easy and a smart buy, but it's best not to put your credit card number into a "public" machine. Use one at home, instead, or call the company on an "800" number, if you found something on the library computer you wanted to buy.

Also be careful of *wireless* internet connections. Sometimes, sitting at that coffee shop with a laptop, while you type your credit card number on that internet web site, software could be catching your keystrokes and saving them for criminals.

When you are standing outside, perhaps using an ATM machine, don't let anyone see you punch your numbers into the machine or look over your shoulder. If you're not comfortable at that machine, stop and use another one later. Pick up mail from your mailbox frequently, especially if it is not locked. Consider getting a post office box that you can unlock and retrieve mail from.

Keep track of the cards you keep in your wallet. Keep a list of all your important identification and credit cards at home so you have all the numbers ready if you have to report your wallet lost or stolen. You'll need a driver's license or I.D. card and a credit card in your wallet, but try to keep your social security card separate if you need to carry it with you.

Opt Out

Here's another important way to keep your personal information from being sold or given away by companies that collect it: **Opt Out**. This is a backward kind of idea, since we might think, "Oh, the bank/credit card company/shoe store will not sell or give away my information unless I say ok." It would be very nice if we were always **asked first** if our information could be sold. It doesn't work that way.

Companies often sell information (like lists of customers and their names, addresses, phone numbers) to other companies. Some of them, like financial institutions, legally have to send us a yearly letter telling us what their policy is for providing other companies access to their databases. Watch for those letters. I know it's boring to read them, but part of what they tell you is how to "Opt Out." They tell you how you can **stop them** from selling or giving away your personal info. Sometimes, they tell you to write them a letter. Sometimes, they give you a form to send back (the nicer ones). Sometimes, there is a telephone number to call or a web site where you can fill out a form. This is a very important way to limit the amount of personal information floating around out there for companies to buy and exploit.

This is not an exhaustive list of ideas to keep you safe, but if you follow these simple steps, you will give anyone who is trying to steal all your numbers a much harder time. It's likely they will give up and move on to an easier target.

"CINDERELLA TAKES CHARGE"

CHAPTER 9

Taking Charge of Your Money

This guide has hopefully given you some basic power to make good decisions and to keep good track of your money in everyday activities. Remember the key words I started with:

Planning = Power = Savings = Financial Health

If you don't feel ready for big changes or you're feeling like there are too many steps all at once, make just one or two changes. Any changes you make can help keep money in your pocket. If you've already gotten into some money trouble, choosing **just** to make sure you have money in the bank means you're avoiding bouncing checks. This **one step** means more power over your money.

Don't give away your power by depending on the bank to know your balance or an adviser to take care of your money without your attention. **You need to be your own adviser and financial planner, first, before anyone else handles your money.** That doesn't mean that you should never seek advice. It means to seek advice and then **monitor** the results. Work **with** an advisor, don't just leave your money unattended. It means checking your investments quarterly to make sure they are earning money. It means balancing your checkbook and spending within your means. In these chapters, I've laid out a system where you can take charge of your own money, watch your budget and never give a bank or credit card company money you don't want them to have.

I feel proud when I know I haven't paid finance charges or late fees. I feel proud that when I buy things on sale, I know they stay at that sale price! I know that I've taken the best care of myself that I can and Planned as well as I'm able with whatever amounts of money I have. I feel proud that my credit score is good enough to get me the best interest rates and I don't have to worry about people calling my house and threatening to turn things off or take things away from me.

I hope you find **fun** in the **Power** to make these decisions. It doesn't have to suck or be an awful chore to balance your checkbook or pay your bills. Even when money has to leave you, you can feel confident that you made **active** decisions about how and when that money is going to go.

Here's to your (financial) health!

Glossary

adult (legal) – any person age 18 years or older as defined by the U.S. federal government of; held responsible for every action taken, including signing contracts or committing illegal conduct, even when the person does not know the conduct is illegal

bankruptcy – legal situation, filed in court, where loans (1) are officially forgiven entirely by the loaners (banks, stores, gas companies) and do not have to be paid back, or (2) where the entire amount of the loan is reduced by agreed upon percentages and only the agreed upon amount is expected to be paid back

before tax/after tax – the timing of when taxes are applied to earnings. Before tax money is money that no taxes are deducted from at that point in time, which is subject to be taxed at a later date. After tax money is money on which taxes have been paid from earnings and no further taxation is necessary in the future.

business day – Mondays through Fridays, excluding federal holidays that fall on any Mondays through Fridays, usually ending at 5:00 or 6:00 p.m. in each time zone

cashing or clearing a check – the moment when money has officially been taken out of a bank account and has been handed to someone in a cash form or transmitted from one bank account to another in electronic form

compound growth – the growth of interest (see compound interest) usually for investment/retirement accounts; applied to investments income, and sometimes referred to as growth over a long term, even when investment accounts sometimes lose money, since the money is expected eventually to increase again, and over time become a steadily increasing amount (presuming it remains in the account)

compound interest – a calculation made where interest money, including fees or interest, is added together with the principal (this action is compounding two into one) and then more fees or interest are charged on top

credit your account – when an agency (bank, store giving a refund, credit card company) gives back your money, not in a cash form, but in an electronic transfer

earned income – money received only from hours worked, excluding money that earns interest from savings or money increases in investment accounts

float a check – the action of writing a check when there is not enough money in an account to pay that check, where an expectation or hope is that other money gets deposited into the account to increase the balance, before this (floated) check is actually cashed or cleared (considered an illegal activity)

grace period – the amount of days a company gives you to make a payment before they add penalties or fees

green card – not actually green in color, a document that allows a non-citizen individual to work in the United States

gross income – all money earned in a calendar year from any source or multiple jobs, before any taxes or other deductions are taken out of it

inflation – used to describe how the dollar you hold today is less able to buy goods in the future if prices rise than that dollar buys today

insufficient funds/nonsufficient funds – not enough money is available in an account to complete the transaction

interest – amount of money charged for the service of using someone else's money, either as a bank gives it to you when the bank borrows/uses your savings or when you give pay fees to the bank when you borrow/use their money for a period of time; meant for transactions where someone does not already personally own all the money that is being used

"matching" percentage or money – an amount of money given to you by someone else that equals the same as the amount of money you are using (for instance, if you put 3% of your paycheck into your retirement account, your employer may match you and give an additional 3% into your retirement account)

net income – the value left of all money earned in a calendar year from any source or multiple jobs, after deducting taxes, fees, retirement or other money from the gross amount

post-date a check – putting a date on the date line of the front (face) of a check that is a day or many days into the future, rather than today's date

principal – the original amount of the loan, with no added fees or amounts

retirement accounts – money that is put aside in specially designated accounts or investments that are covered by special laws and regulations to allow the money to grow over long periods to be used to support a worker when a certain age (such as 59 or 67) is reached and ability to work is diminished

running balance – adding and subtracting each amount of money that goes into or out of a checking account, rather than waiting days or weeks to add or subtract a lot of activities at once

simple interest – a calculation made where fees or interest are calculated only on the cost of the original loan (see principal), without adding prior fees or interest into the calculation

stop check – action a bank takes, usually for a fee, to prevent a check from cashing or clearing from an account

transfer a balance – move the entire amount money in one account or credit card to another

underground economy – exchanging cash for labor or goods without using paperwork, reporting transactions to governmental agencies, or formally recognizing the transactions

Addendum

For More Information On These Topics

Chapter 1: Starting Out — Adult Responsibilities

IRS Forms: www.irs.gov/individuals/index.html

Tax Policy Center: www.taxpolicycenter.org

Chapter 2: Getting a Job

W-4 Form: www.irs.gov/pub/irs-pdf/fw4.pdf

Free W-4 Calculator at PayCheckCity.com:
www.paycheckcity.com/w4/w4instruction.asp

I-9 Form: uscis.gov/graphics/formsfee/forms/files/i-9.pdf

Chapter 3: Keeping Track of Your Money

Federal Reserve Board: www.federalreserve.gov

American Bankers Association: www.aba.com

Consumers Union (publishes "Consumer Reports"):
www.consumersunion.org

Chapter 4: Using Credit Cards

Freddie Mac (Housing Lenders): www.freddiemac.com
"Understanding Credit" and "Credit Smart"

National Foundation for Credit Counseling: 800-388-2227 or
www.nfcc.org

National Consumer Law Center: www.consumerlaw.org

Consumer Federation of America: www.consumerfed.org

Comparing Credit Cards for Best Values: www.cardweb.com;
www.creditcards.com; www.bankrate.com;
moneycentral.msn.com/banking/services/creditcard.asp

Chapter 5: Knowing Your Credit Score

www.howstuffworks.com

Fair, Isaac & Company: www.fairisaac.com

FICO scores: www.myfico.com

Credit Reporting Agencies:

  Experian: www.experian.com or 888-397-3742

  TransUnion: www.transunion.com or 800-888-4213

  Equifax: www.equifax.com or 800-685-1111

Official Site to Order Free Credit Reports:
  www.annualcreditreport.com/cra/index.jsp

To Order Free Credit Reports By Phone: 877–322–8228

Information on Credit Scores: 888-878-3256 or
  www.consumeraction.gov/caw_credit_reports_scores.shtml

Chapter 6: Paying Late – Only When You Have To

Consumers' Rights in dealing with collection agencies –
  Federal Trade Commission: www.ftc.gov/bcp/conline/
  pubs/credit/fdc.htm or 800-FTC-HELP (382-4357)
Negotiate with Lenders – "Knee Deep in Debt":
  www.ftc.gov/bcp/conline/pubs/credit/kneedeep.htm

www.consumer.gov/sentinel

WA State Attorney General: 206-464-6684 or www.atg.wa.gov

Northwest Justice Project: www.nwjustice.org/docs/200.html

Statute of Limitations for Debts: www.fair-debt-collection.com

Credit Counseling Advice:
  Association of Independent Consumer Credit Counseling
  Agencies, www.aiccca.org or National Foundation for Credit
  Counseling, www.nfcc.org

What Questions to Ask Credit Counseling Services Before
  Signing Up: www.ftc.gov/bcp/conline/pubs/credit/fiscal.
  htm

Chapter 7: Saving Through Better Shopping

Research Companies:
  Federal Citizen Information Center, www.pueblo.gsa.gov
  and Consumer Action Handbook, www.consumeraction.gov

Hoover's www.hoovers.com

Thomasnet.com

Coordinated Legal Technologies: www.coordinatedlegal.com

Better Business Bureau: search.bbb.org/search.html

Student Loan Information: www.salliemae.com or Direct Loan
Servicing, www.dlservicer.ed.gov

Chapter 8: Keeping Your Personal Information Safe

Post Office "Vacation Hold" – US Postal Service: 800-275-8777

List of Items to Shred:
www.atg.wa.gov/consumer/idprivacy/priv_shred.shtml

Removing Your Name from Mailing Lists:
888-5-OPTOUT (67-8688) or www.optoutprescreen.com

Direct Marketing Association, Mail Preference Service,
PO Box 9008, Farmingdale, NY 11735-9008 or www.
dmaconsumers.org ($5 fee for online registration)

Reporting Mail Theft: Local Post Office or
www.usps.com/postalinspectors

National Fraud Information Center: 800-876-7060 or make an
online incident report at http://68.166.162.20/repoform.
htm

FTC Identity Theft Hotline: 877-ID-THEFT (438-4338),
www.consumer.gov/idtheft

Identity Theft Resource Center: www.idtheftcenter.org

Index

About the Author

Miryam Gordon lives in Seattle, Washington. She has two adult children, Seth and Magnus Gordon. Helping her children learn to manage their money wisely was a top parental priority. The techniques and tools she developed for them were the inspiration for this book.

Miryam spent over twelve years as the owner of an accounting firm, helping small businesses to manage their money. She became convinced that every person needs a firm foundation in basic money management tools in order to negotiate the world with success.

These days, many people are filing for bankruptcy, hurting financially, and even losing their homes. Even though there are many great money management books, people may be intimidated by them, especially if they're big and heavy. So much information might be overwhelming. She created this book to give people the essentials that can jump-start them to better habits.